Love, Mindset and Multiple Sclerosis

Latecia Tene Pearson

Written Words Publishing LLC
P.O. Box 462622
Aurora, Colorado 80046
www.writtenwordspublishing.com

Published by Written Words Publishing LLC June 28, 2024.

ISBN: 978-1-961610-13-2 (paperback)
ISBN: 978-1-961610-14-9 (eBook)

Library of Congress Control Number: 2024910191

Cover designed by Written Words Publishing LLC

Manufactured and printed in the United States of America

DEDICATION

I dedicate this book to my parents who have shown a wonderful example of how to love in good and bad times.

TABLE OF CONTENTS

ACKNOWLEDGMENTS

I would like to acknowledge my adult children, Janelle and Peyton, for jogging with me through this rocky journey of life.

I would like to thank Rena Phillips for being there in my time of need.

Many thanks to Cassandra Sanders for opening her home to me.

I also thank Camilla Frazier for always having the words from God when they were needed.

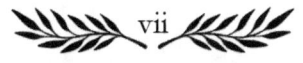

CHAPTER ONE

STRAINING FORWARD

"Brothers and sisters, I do not consider myself yet to have taken hold of it. But one thing I do: Forgetting what is behind and straining toward what is ahead,"
(Philippians 3:13).

In 2009, a neurological condition started attacking my body. I felt like I was going insane and did not know if it was a physical condition or if it was all in my mind. The effects of what I experienced were concerning to say the least. The sporadic fallings were alarming, but not enough in the beginning to go to the hospital. "I'm okay. I'm okay," I'd say as I quickly stood up and brushed myself off then continued to go on my way. It wasn't until the third or fourth fall that raised concern, enough for me to consult my doctor which turned into many visits with various doctors

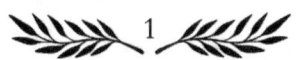

due to the "titles" they put on what I thought was a disease. I was eventually diagnosed with Multiple Sclerosis, also known as MS.

Looking back, I realized that it was caused by my brain being bombarded with events that led me into demeaning thoughts which accelerated my spiral into a black abyss of depression. Three car wrecks within two years caused my insurance to increase resulting in a financial strain. I began dreaming of being chauffeured everywhere I went, which is why I am now more specific in what I pray for.

The third wreck was the nail that initiated the bitter divorce from my husband of twenty-five years. Of course, it was more than the car accidents that sparked the divorce. Although for better or worse are marriage vows, when a couple is figuring out how to succeed in this world, an unexpected, unforeseen disease is a difficult obstacle to overcome. Dealing with MS was not a battle he was willing to take on. It was heartbreaking but I respect him for being able to make that tough decision. Nonetheless, it was a strange time to utter the word "divorce." The timing was terrible but, in hindsight, it was no surprise. Our relationship was awesome but, at times, the word was thrown into the atmosphere.

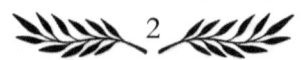

I would dust it off and tell myself that it was just a phase and part of our growth process.

During the divorce proceedings, the MS took a hiatus. It was as if it decided to give me a break, knowing that the division was tough enough. This leads me to believe the disease was triggered by emotions that progressed to my physical being. There's a myriad of reasons why the body attacks itself. Most likely, this is why the medical community has not rendered a cure for MS—medication cannot be used to treat a lack of love.

Self-awareness combined with my connection with God has been my saving grace. Now, I have been slowly restored by giving praises to the Lord every morning, drinking at least one glass of high alkaline water daily, and maintaining a nutritious diet.

Abiding by the Godly instructions which are downloaded to me throughout each day has been the most important factor in my journey. Researching MS on a spiritual, physical and mental level has become my new norm.

CHAPTER TWO

THOUGHTS INTO EXISTENCE

"The weapons we fight with are not the weapons of the world. On the contrary, they have divine power to demolish strongholds" (2 Corinthians 10:4).

While studying MS, it became clear that the disease had not come to take me out. According to God's Word in 1 Peter 5:10, *"…the God of all grace, who called you to his eternal glory in Christ, after you have suffered a little while, will himself restore you and make you strong, firm and steadfast."* This confirms that the journey actually came to make me stronger. I can testify that going through my life's experiences while following the same pattern as many of the depressing thoughts related to my divorce and ailment did indeed strengthen me.

I studied and lived with relapsing-remitting multiple sclerosis which is a disease that damages

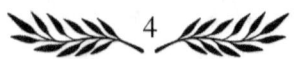

the brain and spinal cord and causes the immune system to attack the myelin (the insulation protecting the nerves), thereby forming scar tissue. When the nerves become damaged, they cannot properly pass along their signals resulting in flare-ups of the disease or relapses. Between these flare-ups, there may be periods of recovery or remissions.

While studying the disease before it was diagnosed, I allowed my thoughts to be consumed by the symptoms, thus correlating what I was thinking and feeling into claiming the disease as mine. By repeatedly associating my thoughts with the declaration, "I probably have multiple sclerosis," I turned it into reality. We have to be careful what we think and speak because, according to Proverbs 18:21, *"The tongue has the power of life and death, and those who love it will eat its fruits."* This ultimately means that what we speak will manifest into existence. I now know that instead of declaring I have MS, I should've been claiming that by His stripes I am healed and made whole according to Isaiah 53:5 and 1 Peter 2:24.

The mental, physical and spiritual responses to my predicament determined the magnitude of my growth. This has truly been a workout for my mind with meditation being the tool for growth,

my body with the proper nutrients as well as exercise building strength in my limbs, and my spirit with prayer and praise which strengthened the faith already within me. This combination is unlike any routine I have ever knowingly experienced. It has given me an increase in consciousness, intelligence, imagination, judgment, memory, and emotion, which is everything the mind is comprised of and are the tools needed to fight all battles within the body.

The lesson in this battle continues to be to focus on keeping my mind on God's Word and making sure my thoughts and desires are in accordance with the desires He has for me. His desires far outweigh anything I can ever dream of.

CHAPTER THREE

TOPSY TURVY

"Therefore this is what the Lord says: 'I will put obstacles before this people. Parents and children alike will stumble over them; neighbors and friends will perish'"
(Jeremiah 6:21).

As if the information within my brain and body were not "misfiring" enough, I had to endure working my way through the realization that I had a disease, along with three faulty car accidents, and a divorce. My saving grace was the God-given adrenaline that He created to take over my body in these fight or flight moments. While the symptoms of MS still remained, they were somewhat more bearable due to other life-altering court business that had to be handled. This showed me that I had control of the disease and, eventually, my healing process would continue.

However, the detour had another purpose, yet to be determined and my back was covered.

In hindsight, 20/20 took over along with approximately ten years of depression until I made the decision one day to be joyful. I became sick and tired of being sick and tired which delivered me into a pleasant state of mind, and thus my next life chapter began. God played a huge part in my mental transition, along with a deep desire to not be an embarrassment to my children who were 17 and 8 years old when I got divorced. My initial thoughts were to protect them from being fatherless and keep my ex-husband in my life, hoping we would get back together. I came to the hurtful realization that wasn't his desire, so I chose to focus on how not to be depressed. That decision made a huge difference in my life. It gave me the revelation that MS could be reversed and the healing process began again.

I dismissed my anger and resentment for the disease, divorce and depression, and blocked all destructive thoughts about any adversities I had to face. I started paying more attention to how those situations were handled, made better choices and practiced self-care. I studied Dr. Sebi's and Ann Boroch's teachings about how to overcome diseases and began taking herbs. This helped my

body stay strong and gave me the desire to focus on how to get my temple in shape.

I now live a steady life according to 1 Corinthians 6:19-20, *"Do you not know that your bodies are temples of the Holy Spirit, who is in you, whom you have received from God? You are not your own; you were bought at a price. Therefore honor God with your bodies."*

CHAPTER FOUR

CHOICES

"Trust in the Lord with all your heart and lean not on your own understanding; in all your ways submit to him, and he will make your paths straight"
(Proverbs 3:5-6).

Choosing to heal is not often thought of. We tend to understandably listen to doctors (words) instead of taking control of our healing powers as powerful humans. Taking healing into our open hands can be done with much prayer, visioning and belief. When I decided to heal, opposition crept in and challenged me, but it did not win the battle. Mind, body and spirit were the keys that opened the door to my healing.

Scripture tells us in Proverbs 17:3 that the Lord tests hearts, essentially, our minds, will and emotions. Losing my apartment and moving in

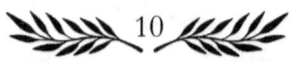

with two strangers didn't go well but I survived, so I would say the test was passed. Thank God, a longtime friend allowed me to move in with her. She questioned why I had not previously contacted her for assistance. My answer was not wanting to be in another county away from my kids. Here lies the next test, should I have shown my appreciation for God or leaned on the notion that I "needed" my kid's help? The answer is quite simple because the Bible tells us, *"Trust in the Lord with all your heart and lean not on your own understanding; in all your ways submit to him, and he will make your paths straight"* (Proverbs 3:5-6). It took a few weeks to recognize the vast blessing in my face, but the gratefulness I felt was overwhelming and my growth during that chapter of life was tremendous. It had a great impact on the beginning of my healing process.

We must be grateful for the opportunities given to us, and when we seek God, our trials will be overcome. For it is written in 1 Peter 4:12-13, *"Dear friends, do not be surprised at the fiery ordeal that has come to test you, as though something strange were happening to you. But rejoice inasmuch as you participate in the sufferings of Christ, so that you may also be overjoyed when his glory is revealed."* In John 16:33, Jesus tells us, *"I have told you these things, so that in me you may have peace. In the world you will have trouble. But take heart! I have overcome the world.* "Romans 8:18 says, *"I consider that our present sufferings are not worth comparing with the glory that will be revealed in us."*

Although my thoughts concerning being alone in my apartment often came to mind, they quickly resolved themselves with the feeling that I was never alone and I began to wonder if my circumstance was a test. After having several roommates that I did not "gel" with, a long-time friend welcomed me into her home to get myself together physically, financially and emotionally, and she is deeply appreciated. My first choice, of course, was having my own place, but I believe we often get exactly what we need and for that I am extremely happy. Although friends and family are important, when I make communicating with the Lord first in my life, I continually see that things are going right. The constant activity of first relating with God has allowed my broken body and spirit to rejuvenate to a point where the healing is physically seen as well as felt. A good support team may not have understood what I was going through, but respecting my decision to handle it and how I'd like to resolve it was vital and I received that support from my friend.

Now, I realize the feelings I've felt about

various people were an emphatic type of energy that not everyone has and it makes sense that the type of person I attract tends to be one that doesn't have my best interest at heart, only theirs. For this reason, my circle of friends remains small.

CHAPTER FIVE

THE CONNECTION OF RENEWING THE MIND

"Do not conform to the pattern of this world, but be transformed by the renewing of your mind…"
(Romans 12:2).

My current circumstances include weakness in my right leg, but I am grateful to God for the ability to still use it. Thank You, God! I'm in a situation that I am so grateful for yet, I would like to own my home and have a partner that loves me unconditionally. My mindset has totally shifted for the better which has given me hope as well as a sense of direction in life. Mental attacks do present themselves in the form of loneliness and depression then tries to creep in. Gladly, it is counteracted with conversations with my Lord who immediately reminds me of the solution,

which is ultimately communicating with the Father and sometimes talking to my roommate. She normally relates or says something that makes me laugh. One of the greatest things is when she shares her writing gift which encourages me to continue to write as well.

My mind is easily distracted when thoughts of what could have been arise. At these times, the best thing I can do for myself is to turn on something funny which distracts my thoughts and gives me that boost needed to continue to enjoy my day. The Bible tells us that a cheerful heart is good medicine (Proverbs 17:22). Laughter can work wonders for the body and it's an amazing tool.

My belief is that the body is regenerative and can be healed of all things with the power within oneself. One way this can be done is by the conversations had with God. The Bible says, "*...in every situation, by prayer and petition, with thanksgiving, present your requests to God. And the peace of God, which transcends all understanding, will guard your hearts and your minds in Christ Jesus*" (Philippians 4:6-7).

Meditating is another way the body calms and sleep is the most regenerative tool that is given to us, in place of evasive surgeries which are popular today.

CHAPTER SIX

SUGAR

*"Have nothing to do with godless myths and old wives'
tales; rather, train yourself to be godly"*
(1 Timothy 4:7).

*"It is not good to eat too much honey, nor is it honorable
to search out matters that are too deep"*
(Proverbs 25:27).

My body was attacking itself and my eating
habits helped fuel the fire. My diet used to consist
of ice cream, sandwiches, packaged foods, and
flavored waters for the sake of "getting my water
in," not to mention snacks, which were eaten as if
they were a fifth food group. The weekly drive-
through to a fast-food restaurant was always
welcomed without realizing the demeaning effect
on my health and well-being. Living to eat instead

of eating to live was my unknown motto.

Our nutritional intake feeds our cells to perform the required daily tasks of living. I now know that fast food does not have the nutrients to aid the body with everyday tasks. This knowledge led to seeking out my first Naturopath. A Naturopath is one who uses natural remedies to help the body heal itself. Naturally, nature has plants which can be used to treat various ailments. There are specialists who have studied the herbs and make it their business to help people heal such as the Yahki Awakened Herbal Store, Dr Sebi and many more which are in my database of herbalists.

My Naturopath was able to detect my food sensitivities and gave me a blueprint for the items that should and should not be consumed. Although reading nutritional labels was not a habit of mine, it quickly became one. Thus far, the natural path has been successful. As I trained my mind to trust in God, I also trained my tastebuds to eat and enjoy the proper nutrients while overcoming MS.

In Genesis 1:29, *"Then God said, 'I give you every seed-bearing plant on the face of the whole earth and every tree that has fruit with seed in it. They will be yours for food.'"* This scripture clearly informs us that natural nutrients and remedies are meant for our bodies.

It provoked me to think about the decisions I made regarding my health. Taking shots of manmade concoctions while doctors tried to figure out how various ailments could be cured was obviously not the right choice. I believe in God's Word, therefore, trying different substances was not the correct way to handle my health issue.

Now, everything that goes in my body is intentionally chosen and researched before being consumed. My nutritional content really increased after seeking out other local Naturopaths who were all able to transfer my body from a constant acid state to an alkaline state. Changing my body to an alkaline state meant shopping at specific stores for organic foods, but even then, some specific foods and recipes had to be followed in order to maintain the newfound state and develop a new palate for those "clean foods." The process and new way of eating has been quite pricey but well worth the investment!

CHAPTER SEVEN

ENERGY

"To this end I strenuously contend with all the energy Christ so powerfully works in me" (Colossians 1:29).

Energy is God and, therefore, what we are. People use this gift in many ways, most for good and some not so good. Either way, we have a power that allows for smiles, growth, joyful skips, and the like. As things unfold, it's a challenge remembering that it's all unfolding for our betterment. According to God's Word, all things work together for the good of those who love Him, who have been called according to His purpose (Romans 8:28).

Sometimes, when my nerves begin to quiver, meditation brings to memory that I have a purpose. Although the disease appears to be a curse, it's a blessing to me and the reason why I continue to smile throughout the challenging moments in this battle.

As my body continues to be borrowed, the knowledge remains that this vessel must be kept in a way that shows appreciation. Anything less is unacceptable and has to be corrected, regardless of how challenging it may be. I am grateful for this entire opportunity.

CHAPTER EIGHT

DECIPHERING DIRECTION

"Keep on loving one another as brothers and sisters"
(Hebrews 13:1).

There are a variety of ways to deal with the choices we make within our bodies. The various alternatives are supposed to be self-regulated to look more like our Creator, who is the epitome of love. This ongoing developmental process is not without pains, but knowing eventually that the procedure will culminate into expansive growth, makes everything worthwhile.

There are many ways of eating. Some people just let their stomach lead while others allow different parts of the body, such as eyes, lead the way. My belief is that there is a right way and a way which leads to a large amount of disaster when people follow the fads that are advertised on

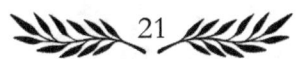

television and other places that promote their way to gain finances.

The Mediterranean Diet, which is popular in countries such as Italy, Greece, Spain, and Israel, enhances one's overall health by reducing the body's intake of red meat, sugar and saturated fat. There is also the Flexitarian Diet which traditionally uses vegetables and the Mayo Clinic Diet which is a 12-week program designed to establish healthy eating habits.

At this point, one can make up a diet which consists of other ways of eating to try staving off disease according to how their body reacts to the foods and put a name on it. Diets tend to be a trend; some are needed and others simply support those who desire a change in eating habits. Either way, these much-needed nutrients, termed diets, are vital to our bodies, providing the cells with necessary nutrients to help us move through the day. Done right, they will keep enemies, such as obesity or malnutrition, away.

It takes self-discipline to stick to a nutritional diet. *"No discipline seems pleasant at the time, but painful. Later on, however, it produces a harvest of righteousness and peace for those who have been trained by it"* (Hebrews 12:11). Although it may seem difficult and painful at first, the end result will be well worth it.

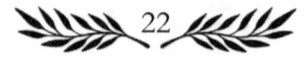

Typically, once someone practices the same routine for 30 days or more, it becomes a habit. One way a person can adopt a nutritional habit is by fasting and praying. Start with a Daniel Fast which consists of only eating fruits and vegetables and drinking water for 21-days while praying daily to seek guidance from God.

CHAPTER NINE

POWER

"For the Spirit God gave us does not make us timid, but give us power, love and self-discipline" (2 Timothy 1:7).

The mind and brain are two separate portions within our absolute joy. The mind uses the brain to control and display our thoughts, feelings and emotions, both consciously and unconsciously. The brain is an organ that regulates and manages how the body functions. Although my myelin sheaths were not functioning properly, it was vital that the protection of my nerves worked conjunctively along with my thoughts.

And praise, at all times, is critical. It was not my way of handling the issues that came into my world, but I had no choice but to change. The power is within me to strengthen my mind, body and soul.

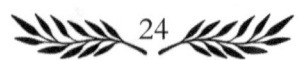

The Bible tells us, with the knowledge of God, we can be *"…strengthened with all power according to his glorious might so that you may have great endurance and patience"* (Colossians 1:11). Therefore, praising God, giving Him all the glory, and exercise has become a daily routine to keep myself from becoming stagnant and worthless.

According to Proverbs 23:7, we are what we think. That encouraging scripture continues to give me the hope needed to use the power that has been given to me, as well as the energy in the foods of this earth, to heal my body. Being fed by the reports of this world along with following the mindset of those around is not the choice I've made for my life. At the moment, it may look bleak, but using the power within me to continuously renew my mind helps to keep the momentum of my gift called life.

Chapter Ten

Decisions

"Therefore, I urge you, brothers and sisters, in view of God's mercy, to offer your bodies as a living sacrifice, holy and pleasing to God—this is your true and proper worship. Do not conform to this world, but be transformed by the renewing of your mind. Then you will be able to test and approve what God's will is—his good, pleasing and perfect will" (Romans 12:1-2).

My kids live with my ex-husband, so the struggle of feeling that I lost that battle bothers me a couple of times a week. The lessons I've learned while dealing with MS have helped me overcome the thought of loss when it appears. I have been able to use the following methods to feel good again after our separation:

1. Planning luncheons.
2. Thanking God for their life, as well as mine.

3. Believing joy will find me as I continue to seek it.

My mindset has totally shifted which has given me hope and a sense of direction in life. Mental attacks do present themselves in the form of loneliness, but they are counteracted by a conversation with my Lord who immediately gives me a solution, which is usually as simple as a friend or one of my kids randomly calling and wanting to get me out of my apartment or involved with a crypto currency venture, which is a passion of mine. My "tribe" is amazing and has been with me throughout this journey.

Having trust in God and communicating with the Lord allows my broken body and heart to rejuvenate to a point where the healing is physically seen as well as felt.

My connection with God and my belief in the power that was given to me is what keeps the ever-renewing strength that I have alive. So today, I am being restored slowly and I give praise to the Lord for being my strength as I allow my body to be healed by obeying God and following His Word.

Today, my journey continues and there is a lot I plan to accomplish. My thoughts are secured, although tested frequently. My body is still in the progress of recovering and the one thing that has been secured is God's Word. Thus far undoing! The saga continues, but the fact remains, I have MS and it doesn't have me!

ABOUT THE AUTHOR

Latecia Tene Pearson lives in North Hollywood, CA and has two children. She has realized that her children will never be lost because they have been raised to know, honor and love God which will always be a reminder of what's true and what's good. Holding this thought helps her to remain positive and look forward to their time together. They are now adults who are making the positive moves they were taught to make, so the only thing that needs to be found is time—the time which was lost grieving something that could've changed with simple eating habits.

Multiple sclerosis has been a great gift of learning what Latecia should have been taught all those years in school. She now knows the importance of loving yourself first. Doing so, no one or nothing will ever be able to bring her harm.

www.ingramcontent.com/pod-product-compliance
Lightning Source LLC
Chambersburg PA
CBHW070957120626
46546CB00004B/1653